Desktop

TETHERBALL

T0364002

A Popular Pastime

Show of hands: back in elementary school, did you play tetherball?

Did you grab that be-roped ball, then smack it around a metal pole until the rope was wrapped too tightly to allow for further smacking?

Whoa. Lots of hands.

Okay, another show of hands: how many of you, in the midst of a gripping tetherball contest, were whupped upside your head by that aforementioned be-roped ball?

Once again, lots of hands.

A tetherball to the schnozz was the surest way to end an epic t-ball contest—the ecstasy of tether quashed by the agony of getting bopped in the noodle.

Well, there's some good news for tetherball lovers who don't love tetherball-related injuries:

Desktop Tetherball is now available for those who crave a fun, engaging, and injury-free afternoon of t-ball.

But before we dive into Desktop Tetherball, let's go back to where it all began: The Fifth Century.

FUN FACT

A regulation
tetherball pole is ten
feet high. A regulation
desktop tetherball
pole isn't.

The Real
History
of Real
Tetherball

For years, tetherball purists have thumbed their nose at Desktop Tetherball, citing the fact that its lack of history—its Johnny-come-lately-ness, if you will—diminishes its legitimacy.

Admittedly, Desktop Tetherball doesn't have real tetherball's rich backstory, but that's primarily because when real tetherball was alleged to have been invented, desktop games weren't a thing.

According to the *Play and Playground Encyclopedia*—which is a thing—some believe that the roots of tetherball were sown in England, circa 1450, when maypole dancing was all the rage, a time when, " . . . villagers would hold ropes or ribbons hung from a tall pole and dance around the pole." A reasonable, if oddly-worded theory, but *Play and Playground Encyclopedia*'s assertion that tetherball was really invented soon after volleyball, which was created in 1895, rings a bit more true.

Today, tetherball is as popular as it's ever been. According to the National Center for Education Statistics, there are 98,271 public elementary schools in the United States, and it's fair to assume that we can claim an average of one functional tetherball pole per facility. The NCES also tells

FUN FACT

According to Lifetime.com, it's possible to burn 136 calories in one hour of playing real tetherball. Though not yet scientifically proven, it's been guesstimated that it's possible to burn 24 calories in one hour of playing Desktop Tetherball . . . the equivalent of half a chicken wing.

us there are approximately 35.4 million students attending these schools, so even if just half of them are smacking the ball around that pole, tetherball still counts as one of the most popular outdoor activities in the USA.

But what about Desktop Tetherball?

Well, we can only speculate.

The
Official Rules
of
Desktop
Tetherball

(Standard two-player version)

1. Assemble the D.T. set by screwing the bottom piece of the pole into the base, and then screw the metal piece with the string and ball on top. Place on a clear, clutter-free desk or table.

2. Opponents sit in chairs facing one another on opposite sides of the pole, both hands resting palm down on the desktop, one inch away from the pole.

3. In unison, the opponents count to three. Upon saying the number three, the opponents reach for the pole with their dominant index finger. The first to touch the pole is the first to serve.

4. Before the initial service, each player must choose which hand they will be using for the game. Once the hand is declared, the opposite hand is out of play, the only exception being in the event of a severe injury.

5. The ball must be served with a flick of either the index or middle finger. After the service, all fingers are in play, save for the thumb. Utilizing a thumb results in a for-feit of the game, while utilizing a palm, a knuckle, or a fist results in a lifetime D.T. ban.

FUN FACT

According to NBC News,
in 2012, seven-year-old second
grader Ruby Harris defeated
Olympic fencer Jimmy Moody in a
game of real tetherball.

According to eyewitness
accounts, days after writing
this book, the author's four-year-
old daughter defeated him
in a game of Desktop
Tetherball.

6. The ball is flicked until the rope is wrapped around the pole to the point it can be flicked no more.

7. The contest can be decided in two games out of three, or four games out of seven, or 500,001 games out of 1,000,000.

Fun
Variations
on the
Game

Nobody can or will dispute that your garden variety Desktop Tetherball contest is gripping, enticing, and, if played well, exhausting. But there are a number of variations on the sport that are equally as enjoyable if you'd like to try your hand at them:

NOSEBALL

Hands, fingers, and thumbs are all fine and good, but utilizing your schnozz takes the game to a whole new level. The rules are simple: place your Desktop Tetherball pole on the center of a chair, kneel down, then, facing your opponent, rest your chin on the chair, lean your face towards the pole, and get balling! (This variation is strenuous on the neck, so please consult your physician before teeing it up.)

TONGUE TWISTER

A variation on the variation, if you will. The playing position is identical to noseball, but the tongue is your weapon. Please, please, please brush your teeth before playing.

HEADERBALL

Who needs a desktop when you have somebody else's head? Find a friend with a flat, preferably bald or shaven head and an endless well of patience, have them kneel on the floor in between you and your opponent, then tape the Desktop Tetherball pole onto their dome and let it rip. Note: Your smooth-headed pal is doing you a huge favor, so if you feel the urge to pump your fist after a particularly good round, don't do so in your friend's direction.

Those variations are full of tetherbally goodness, no doubt, but the end of the day, it's all about the original, the classic, the game that, one day, will overtake baseball as our Great American Pastime.

After only a few minutes of smacking around your Desktop Tetherball, you'll realize that, despite its diminutive size, the thing packs a huge wallop. It's only a matter of time before the world catches on.

This book has been bound
using handcraft methods and
Smyth-sewn to ensure
durability.

The cover and interior
was illustrated and designed
by Jason Kayser.

The text was written by
Alan Goldsher.